D0243042

THE BUTLER DID IT
AND OTHER PLAYS

Things go wrong, and funny things happen, in these six short plays. There is always something which causes problems for someone.

James, the butler, always does what 'sir' tells him. 'Very good, sir,' he says. That's what makes him a good butler. But one day 'sir' asks James to do something very unusual. Does James do it or not?

Most office workers do what their employer tells them, too. They know exactly what people must or must not do. 'Rules are rules,' they say. This makes life difficult for the man with the monkey, when he visits the licensing office!

Roger's problem is that he hasn't got much money. His rich girlfriend's problem is that he hasn't asked her to marry him. There seems to be an easy answer, but as in all these plays, things are more difficult, and much funnier, than that.

OXFORD BOOKWORMS LIBRARY

Playscripts

The Butler Did It and Other Plays

Stage 1 (400 headwords)

Playscripts Series Editor: Clare West

BILL BOWLER

The Butler Did It

and Other Plays

Retold by
Clare West

OXFORD UNIVERSITY PRESS

OXFORD

UNIVERSITY PRESS

Great Clarendon Street, Oxford OX2 6DP

Oxford University Press is a department of the University of Oxford.
It furthers the University's objective of excellence in research, scholarship,
and education by publishing worldwide in

Oxford New York

Auckland Cape Town Dar es Salaam Hong Kong Karachi
Kuala Lumpur Madrid Melbourne Mexico City Nairobi
New Delhi Shanghai Taipei Toronto

With offices in

Argentina Austria Brazil Chile Czech Republic France Greece
Guatemala Hungary Italy Japan Poland Portugal Singapore
South Korea Switzerland Thailand Turkey Ukraine Vietnam

OXFORD and OXFORD ENGLISH are registered trade marks of
Oxford University Press in the UK and in certain other countries

This simplified edition © Oxford University Press 2008

Database right Oxford University Press (maker)

First published in Oxford Bookworms 2001

4 6 8 10 9 7 5 3

Any websites referred to in this publication are in the public domain and
their addresses are provided by Oxford University Press for information only.
Oxford University Press disclaims any responsibility for the content

ISBN 978 0 19 423535 8

A complete recording of this Bookworms edition of
The Butler Did It and Other Plays is available on audio CD ISBN 978 0 19 423505 1

Printed in China

Illustrated by: Rowan Barnes Murphy

For more information on the Oxford Bookworms Library,
visit www.oup.com/bookworms

CONTENTS

INTRODUCTION

Henry Fletcher is working in his office. He is thinking about his wife. What's she doing at the moment? Has she got a boyfriend? Perhaps she has, perhaps she hasn't. Is she with her lover now? He wants to know! So he phones home. But only James, the butler, answers . . .

CHARACTERS IN THE PLAY

James, a butler
Henry Fletcher, a husband

PERFORMANCE NOTES

There are two rooms on the stage, with a wall between them. One is a dining room, where James the butler is getting the table ready for dinner. There is a telephone in the room. The other room is an office, where Henry Fletcher is working. He is sitting in front of his computer, but he isn't looking at it. He is making a phone call.

You will need two telephones and a gun.

The plumber's name, Blessiu, sounds like 'Bless you!' which is what we often say when someone sneezes.

The Butler Did It

The phone rings in the dining room. James stops work and answers it.

JAMES   Hello.

HENRY   Hello, is that James, the butler?

JAMES   Yes, sir, it is.

HENRY   James, is my wife at home?

JAMES   Yes, sir.

HENRY   Good. Can you bring her to the phone? I want to speak to her at once. Be quick!

JAMES   Very good, sir. So you want me to bring your wife to the phone. Is that right, sir?

HENRY   Yes, yes, James. Now just go and do it. (*James goes off slowly. Henry speaks to himself.*) My wife's got a lover, I think. But I must know! What's James doing? And where's my wife?

James comes back slowly and speaks into the phone.

JAMES   Hello, sir. James speaking.

HENRY   Hello, James. So where's my wife?

JAMES   Your wife is at home, sir, but she can't speak to you at the moment, I'm afraid.

HENRY   She can't speak to me! My wife can't speak to me! Why not?

1

JAMES   Well, sir, she's in the bathroom...

HENRY   In the bathroom!

JAMES   ...with a man.

HENRY   (*Putting a hand to his head*) With a man!

JAMES   But don't worry, sir, it's only Mr Blessiu, the plumber. He's working in the bathroom.

HENRY   (*Not listening, speaking to himself*) She's in the bathroom with her boyfriend! I knew it! James, can you do something for me?

JAMES   Of course, sir.

HENRY   Go into my bedroom, and find the box under my bed. In that box there's a gun. Take it out, James.

JAMES   Very good, sir. You want me to go into your bedroom, find the box under your bed, and take out the gun. Is that right, sir?

HENRY   Yes, James, yes! Just go and do it.

James goes off slowly. Henry speaks to himself.

HENRY   I knew it! My wife's got a lover! But soon James is going to come back with that gun, and then...

James comes back with the gun.

JAMES   (*Into the phone*) Hello, sir, James here.

HENRY   Hello, James. Have you got the gun?

JAMES   Yes, sir. I went into your bedroom, found the box under your bed, and took out the gun. I have it with me now, sir.

HENRY   Right, James. Now listen carefully.

'Hello, sir, James here.'

JAMES   I'm listening very carefully, sir.

HENRY   Go into the bathroom...

JAMES   Yes, sir.

HENRY   ...with the gun...

JAMES   Yes, sir.

HENRY   ...and shoot my wife through the head.

JAMES   Yes, sir.

HENRY   And the man in the bathroom with her, James, shoot him through the head too. (*He sneezes.*)

JAMES   Blessiu, sir?

HENRY   Thank you, James. Now, James, do you

'Did you hear the shots, sir?'

understand what to do?

JAMES   Yes, sir. You want me to go into the bathroom with the gun, shoot your wife through the head, and shoot the man with her through the head, too, sir. (*He sneezes.*)

HENRY   Bless you, James!

JAMES   That's right, sir.

HENRY   Very good, James. Well, just go and do it.

James goes off. We hear two gun shots.

HENRY   (*Looking pleased and smiling to himself*) Aha! Good old James! Well done!

James comes back slowly, without the gun.

JAMES   (*Into the phone*) Hello, sir. Did you hear the shots, sir?

HENRY Yes, James, I did. Is everything all right?

JAMES Oh yes, sir. I went into the bathroom with the gun, and I shot your wife through the head, and I shot the man with her through the head, too.

He sneezes.

HENRY Bless you, James!

JAMES That's right, sir.

HENRY Right, and are the two of them dead, James?

JAMES Oh yes, sir.

HENRY Very good, James. Oh, and James...

JAMES Yes, sir?

HENRY What did you do with the gun?

JAMES The gun, sir?

HENRY Yes, James, the gun. What did you do with it?

JAMES Ah, yes, sir. I put it in the swimming pool.

HENRY The swimming pool, James?

JAMES The swimming pool in the back garden, sir.

HENRY (*Looking afraid*) But we haven't got a swimming pool in our back garden!

Nobody says anything for a moment.

JAMES Oh, I see. Well, then, you've got the wrong number, I'm afraid, sir. Goodbye.

HENRY Oh, I – er – Goodbye.

James goes back to his work, getting the table ready for dinner. He is smiling and singing quietly to himself. Henry sits in his chair, with a very white face.

INTRODUCTION

Celia is sitting at a street café one day, drinking coffee, when suddenly she sees an old school friend, Amanda. The two women are happy to talk about old times and the men in their lives. They always like very different men, of course . . .

CHARACTERS IN THE PLAY

Celia, a woman of about 45
Amanda, her school friend
Waiter
Robert, a man of about 45

PERFORMANCE NOTES

The scene is a street café. There are tables and chairs outside. The waiter sometimes comes out of the café to see if anyone wants anything. Celia is sitting at one of the tables. She is wearing a big, expensive ring on the ring finger of her left hand. You will need a cup of coffee, a bottle or glass of coke, and Celia's ring.

Old Friends

Amanda is walking past the café. Celia suddenly sees her and calls to her.

CELIA   Amanda? Is it you?

AMANDA   Sorry? Do I know you?

CELIA   Of course you do. It's me, Celia. We were at school together.

AMANDA   Celia! How wonderful to see you again!

CELIA   Do you remember me now?

AMANDA   Oh yes, but you do look different.

CELIA   Older, perhaps?

AMANDA   Well, yes.

CELIA   Well, I *am* older! So are you! Sit down and have a drink with me.

AMANDA   Yes, why not? (*She sits down at the table.*)

CELIA   What are you going to have? Coffee?

AMANDA   Oh, a coke, I think.

CELIA   (*Calling*) Waiter! (*The waiter comes to the table.*)

WAITER   Good morning. What would you like?

CELIA   A coffee for me, please, and a coke for my friend.

WAITER   Would you like a sandwich or anything? They're very good.

CELIA   No, no, thank you. Just the drinks.

WAITER Right. (*He goes off.*)

AMANDA Well, this *is* nice! When did we last meet? About fifteen years ago, was it?

CELIA Twenty-five, Amanda.

AMANDA Twenty-five? No! It can't be! Do you sometimes see any of our old friends?

CELIA No, no, I don't.

The waiter brings the drinks and puts them on the table.

WAITER Here you are, one coffee and one coke.

AMANDA (*To him*) Thank you. (*To Celia*) I say, do you remember Rod Hunk? All the girls liked him! What happened to him, do you think?

CELIA Oh, I don't know. I didn't like him much. But what about Rocky Rambo? You and he were together at one time, I think.

AMANDA Ah yes, but he left me years ago.

CELIA Oh, I *am* sorry.

AMANDA No, no, I was happy when he left. I was tired of him, you know. It's always much better to find a new boyfriend! Much more exciting!

CELIA Perhaps you're right. And what about Romeo Valentine? You went out with him, too.

AMANDA Oh yes, but *I* left *him*. Time for a change, I thought!

CELIA Oh, I see.

AMANDA And what about you, Celia? Are there any men in your life at the moment?

'Are there any men in your life at the moment?'

CELIA   (*Looking shyly down at the big expensive ring on her finger*) Well . . .

AMANDA Oh, Celia, do tell me!

CELIA   Well, there *is* a man in my life, and I'm going to marry him next week!

AMANDA You're going to marry him! Wonderful! Tell me all about him.

CELIA   He's called Robert. He's very handsome, but very shy. He's coming here soon, to meet me.

AMANDA His name's Robert? Well, well, well! You know, *I* met a very handsome man last night, and he was called Robert, too. But he wasn't shy! Not at all! He asked me to call him Bob.

'Oh, we had a wonderful time!'

CELIA   *My* Robert doesn't like the name Bob.

AMANDA   Well, I met this Bob in a café and we had a few drinks. And then we went out to dinner. And then we went dancing. Oh, we had a wonderful time!

CELIA   *My* Robert doesn't like dancing.

AMANDA   We talked and laughed and danced, and drank and danced and laughed, and then . . . But what about you and Robert? What do you usually do?

CELIA   Oh well, Robert likes a quiet evening with me at my house. We read, and watch television. Sometimes we go out to the cinema.

AMANDA   Do you? Bob wants to see me again next week. He calls me Mandy. I like that.

CELIA   Robert isn't interested in drinking or dancing or meeting girls. He's a very quiet person.

AMANDA   Bob isn't quiet. Not at all!

CELIA   I'm his first girlfriend, you see. So this is all new to him. Oh look, here he comes now!

Robert comes in, from behind Amanda. He can't see her face. He kisses Celia.

ROBERT   Hello, Celia, darling!

CELIA   Robert, darling! I'd like you to meet an old school friend. Amanda, this is Robert.

ROBERT   How do you do?

AMANDA   How do you do? (*Looking up into his face*) Oh no! It's you! Bob!

ROBERT   (*Seeing her face*) Oh no! It's you! Mandy!

CELIA   (*Angrily*) Robert!

ROBERT   What can I say? I'm sorry! I'm very, very sorry!

Robert runs off. Celia and Amanda run after him.

AMANDA   Bob! Bob! We must talk about all this! I want to see you again!

CELIA   Robert! Robert! Come back here at once! Are you going to marry me or not?

ROBERT   Help! Help! Help!

The waiter comes in.

WAITER   Would you like to pay now? (*He sees them running away.*) Hey, come back!

He runs angrily after them.

INTRODUCTION

Fred Fish isn't happy with his life. He would like to do something more exciting. What's going to happen to him in the future? Perhaps Madame Rosa can tell him. She can read the future in her crystal ball, or in people's hands. Sometimes she can read people's faces, and then she tells them what they want to hear. But sometimes she gets it wrong, and people don't like what she tells them. If they aren't happy, they don't give her any money. And she needs the money.

CHARACTERS IN THE PLAY

Madame Rosa, a woman who can see into the future
Fred Fish, a teacher

PERFORMANCE NOTES

The scene is Madame Rosa's living room, with a table and two chairs. On the table is a big crystal ball. Madame Rosa is sitting at the table, looking into the crystal ball.
You will need a crystal ball and some money.

Fred's Future

ROSA *(Looking into her crystal ball)* What's going to happen today? Ah, I can see money! Yes, somebody's going to give me a lot of money! Wonderful! Who can it be?

FRED *(Coming in)* Hello. Are you Madame Rosa?

ROSA That's right. Do sit down.

Fred sits down at the table.

FRED Thank you. Er, my name's Fred Fish—

ROSA Let me see, you're a teacher, you live in London, and you want to know about your future. Right?

FRED Yes, yes! How do you know all this?

ROSA *(Looking into the crystal ball)* I can see you here.

FRED Wow! That's interesting! So can you tell me about my future? What's going to happen to me?

ROSA I can tell you, but remember, nothing is free these days.

FRED Oh, I know. I brought some money with me.

ROSA *(Smiling)* That's very good! Right, can you give me your hand, please? I'm going to read it. *(She takes his hand and looks carefully at it.)* I can see love here. Soon you're going to meet a beautiful American girl. You're going to marry her.

FRED But I've got a very nice girlfriend at the moment!

She's Australian!

ROSA Forget about her! No, you're going to marry the American. I can see it in your hand.

FRED Can you tell me any more?

ROSA Yes. Soon you're going to leave London and move to Hollywood, with your American wife.

FRED Hollywood! Where all the famous people live!

ROSA That's right. And you're going to stop teaching. You're going to be an actor, and become famous for acting in all the best Hollywood films!

FRED Wonderful! I'm going to become rich!

ROSA Well, yes, but things aren't going to be easy for you. Your wife is going to take a lover.

FRED Oh no! Another famous actor, perhaps?

ROSA Yes, that's right. And you're going to start drinking, at first in the evening, and then in the daytime.

FRED Oh dear, that's bad.

ROSA Yes. And nobody's going to give you any more acting work, because you drink.

FRED So what happens to me after all this?

ROSA You kill yourself, I'm sorry to say.

FRED What? No! I'm not going to kill myself!

ROSA It's very quick. You shoot yourself one night.

FRED I didn't come here to hear about dying!

ROSA It's all in your hand. That's £25, please.

'I didn't come here to hear about dying!'

FRED   It can't be right! Can you look at my hand again?

ROSA   Oh, all right. (*Looking at his hand again*) Let me see – perhaps you marry the *Australian* girl.

FRED   That's better!

ROSA   Yes, and you leave London to move to Sydney, with your Australian wife.

FRED   Mmm, yes, it's wonderfully hot there.

ROSA   And you're going to stop teaching, and become a very good tennis player.

FRED   I was very good at tennis at school, you know.

ROSA   You're going to meet all the famous players and play tennis with them. People are going to watch you playing tennis on TV.

FRED   Wow! I'm going to become rich and famous!

'You're going to become a very good tennis player.'

ROSA   Yes, but things aren't going to be easy for you. Your wife's going to—

FRED   Be careful!

ROSA   Let me see – er – your hand's difficult to read. Ah yes, your wife's going to have a baby.

FRED   Oh, good. I like children.

ROSA   Yes, and then she's going to have a second baby, and then a third.

FRED   Oh! But I'm never going to see the children! I'm going to be on TV all the time!

ROSA   Things aren't going to be easy. I told you that.

FRED   Perhaps I'm going to stop being a tennis player and be a teacher again. Then I can help my wife with the children in the holidays.

ROSA   Er – that's right. It's all in your hand. You're going to stop playing tennis and begin teaching again.

FRED   But am I going to be happy? That's the most important thing.

ROSA   Oh yes. You're going to be very happy with your family, and you're going to live in a beautiful big house in Sydney.

FRED   I can always play tennis with my friends at the weekend.

ROSA   Yes, of course. So there you are. Now you know about your future. Are you happy with that?

FRED   Yes. Yes, thank you. Very interesting. I'm going to ask my girlfriend to marry me at once!

ROSA   Why not? And move to Australia?

FRED   That's right. And before we go, I'm going to play some tennis. I must get better at it!

ROSA   Right, well, that's £30, please.

FRED   Of course. Here you are. (*He takes some money from his pocket and gives it to her.*) Things are going to be very exciting for me! Thank you, thank you, thank you!

ROSA   (*Smiling*) Thank *you*.

She takes the money and Fred goes out.

INTRODUCTION

Mr and Mrs Boggis want a holiday, but they don't know where to go. There are a lot of different places, and it's important to find the right one. Can the travel agent help? She knows all about the different places. Or does she?

CHARACTERS IN THE PLAY

Travel agent, a young woman
Mr Boggis, a man of about 40
Mrs Boggis, his wife
Man who speaks to the audience

PERFORMANCE NOTES

The scene is a travel agent's office, with pictures of holiday places on the walls. The travel agent is sitting at her computer, with two chairs in front of her.
You will need a pen and paper, and some plane tickets.

Have a Nice Holiday!

Mr and Mrs Boggis come into the office.

AGENT Good afternoon. Can I help you?

MR BOGGIS Yes, please. We'd like a holiday.

AGENT Oh, yes. Where would you like to go?

MR BOGGIS What do you think, dear?

MRS BOGGIS Somewhere exciting!

MR BOGGIS *(To the agent)* Somewhere exciting.

AGENT *(Writing it down)* Somewhere exciting.

MRS BOGGIS Somewhere hot!

MR BOGGIS *(To the agent)* Somewhere hot.

AGENT *(Writing it down)* Somewhere hot.

MRS BOGGIS Somewhere far away!

MR BOGGIS *(To the agent)* Somewhere far away.

AGENT *(Writing it down)* Somewhere far away.

MRS BOGGIS And somewhere cheap!

MR BOGGIS *(To the agent)* And somewhere cheap.

AGENT *(Writing it down)* And somewhere cheap. Right, let's see. There's a very nice holiday for two in Florida, in a really good hotel.

MRS BOGGIS Ooh, that's nice!

MR BOGGIS Yes. Very hot, Florida.

MRS BOGGIS Yes, and very exciting.

'Ooh, that's nice!'

MR BOGGIS How much is the Florida holiday?

AGENT Er, let me see. £2,000 for one person...

MR BOGGIS £2,000 for one person!

AGENT ... for one day.

MR BOGGIS For one day!

MRS BOGGIS Oh dear. That's £28,000 for the two of us for a week. That's very expensive.

AGENT You can't have everything. It's a very nice holiday. But let's find something cheaper, shall we?

MR BOGGIS Er, yes, please.

AGENT What about this? A camping holiday for two near the Scott Hills.

MRS BOGGIS Ooh, that's interesting. I like camping. Are they far away, the Scott Hills?

AGENT   Oh, yes, very far away.

MR BOGGIS   Good. And is it a cheap holiday?

AGENT   Oh, yes. Only £20 for each person for a month.

MRS BOGGIS   And is it nice and hot there?

AGENT   Well, not very hot.

MRS BOGGIS   Tell me, where are the Scott Hills?

AGENT   In Antarctica, near the South Pole.

MR BOGGIS   Near the South Pole! But that isn't hot.

AGENT   No, but it's a very cheap holiday. I told you, you can't have everything.

MR BOGGIS   Look, we want somewhere hot *and* cheap.

AGENT   OK. Well, this one's just right for you.

MRS BOGGIS   Is it cheap?

AGENT   Oh, yes. It's cheap. Only £200 for two people. That's very cheap.

MR BOGGIS   Is it somewhere hot?

AGENT   Oh, yes. It's hot. But it isn't very far away, I'm afraid.

MRS BOGGIS   Oh, that doesn't matter. Where is it?

AGENT   Margarita, in the south of Spain. The Hotel Fantastico is very quiet, only five minutes' walk to the sea, and it has a swimming pool.

MRS BOGGIS   Ooh, that's wonderful. Let's take it.

MR BOGGIS   Yes, let's! Can I pay for it now? And can we go tomorrow?

AGENT   Of course. (*She takes Mr Boggis's money and*

gives him two tickets.) Here are your tickets. Have a nice holiday! Goodbye!

MR AND MRS BOGGIS   Thank you. Goodbye!

Mr and Mrs Boggis go out with their tickets. A man comes in and speaks to the audience.

MAN   So, Mr and Mrs Boggis are going to have a wonderful holiday, are they? What do you think? Let's see, shall we? It's now two weeks later.

He goes off. Mr and Mrs Boggis come into the travel agent's office.

AGENT   Good morning. Can I help you?

MR BOGGIS   We're very angry about one of your holidays. To Margarita, it was.

AGENT   Ah, yes. Cheap, hot, and not very far away.

MR BOGGIS   Well, Margarita was OK, but the hotel was no good at all. It was quiet, you said.

AGENT   Well, I did say that, yes.

MRS BOGGIS   Well, the building was only half finished, so there were men at work day and night! There was a lot of noise.

MR BOGGIS   We couldn't sleep at all.

MRS BOGGIS   And it had a swimming pool, you said.

AGENT   Well, er, yes, perhaps I did say that.

MR BOGGIS   That was half finished, too. No water in it.

AGENT   I see. Well—

MRS BOGGIS   Five minutes' walk to the sea, you said.

'We're very angry about one of your holidays!'

MR BOGGIS Perhaps it takes five minutes in a taxi. Not on foot, oh no!

AGENT Oh dear. Well, I'm very sorry. Perhaps you'd like some of your money back?

MRS BOGGIS No, we'd like another holiday now.

AGENT Oh, yes, why not? How about two plane tickets to Australia? It's exciting, hot and very far away!

MRS BOGGIS Ooh, wonderful! Let's take them.

AGENT Here are your tickets, then. Have a nice holiday!

They go out happily with their tickets.

AGENT (*Smiling*) The tickets are only *to* Australia! Perhaps they're never going to come back!

INTRODUCTION

A man wants to keep an animal in his house. It isn't a cat or a dog, but a monkey. He needs a licence for the monkey, so he goes to the office which gives out licences. But people who work in offices like having rules, and rules cannot be broken. So getting a licence is more difficult than the man thought.

CHARACTERS IN THE PLAY

Woman who works in the office
Man with a monkey

PERFORMANCE NOTES

The scene is an office. There is a sign that says ROOM 365 on the wall. There are three chairs near the door, and a table and two chairs in the middle of the room. There is a telephone on the table. A woman is sitting writing at the table. A man is waiting at the open door. He is carrying a monkey.

You will need a telephone, two numbered tickets, some photos, a sign saying ROOM 563, a sign saying ROOM 365, and a monkey.

Rules are Rules

WOMAN (*Not looking up*) Come in.

MAN (*Coming in*) Good morning.

The woman is writing. She doesn't answer.

MAN Hello – er – Excuse me.

WOMAN (*Looking up angrily*) Have you got a number?

MAN Sorry?

WOMAN You can get a ticket with a number outside the door. Before you come in. Have you got a number?

MAN (*Looking round*) But there's no one here. Only me! So I don't need a number, do I?

WOMAN That doesn't matter. Everybody must have a number. (*She begins writing again.*)

MAN Oh, I see. All right. (*He goes out.*)

WOMAN (*Without looking up*) Number 68. (*She waits a minute.*) Number 69. (*She waits.*) Number 70.

The man comes back with his ticket.

MAN I've got my number now.

WOMAN (*Looking up angrily*) Can you wait over there please! Sit on one of those chairs near the door!

MAN But—

WOMAN I have work to do, I'm afraid. Please wait.

The man goes to sit near the door. The woman makes a phone call.

'Wonderful! Goodbye, darling!'

WOMAN   Hello, Tom. It's Pam. I'm calling from work. You're having dinner at my house today, remember? Wonderful! Goodbye, darling!

She calls out numbers, without looking up, and waits for a minute between the numbers.

WOMAN   Number 71. Number 72. Number 73. (*Looking at the man*) What number have you got?

MAN   89.

WOMAN   Oh, you're going to wait a long time, then.

MAN   But why? There's no one here! Why must I wait?

WOMAN   Rules are rules, sir. (*Calling out numbers again*) Number 74. Number 75. Number 76.

MAN   Wait a minute!

WOMAN   You must wait for your number, sir.

MAN But you called my number! Just now!

WOMAN No, I called 76 and your number's 89.

MAN No, no, it isn't. I was wrong. Look! It isn't 89, it's 68! (*He turns his ticket the other way up.*)

WOMAN But I'm on 76 now. Why didn't you answer when I called your number?

MAN I'm sorry. I didn't know. But I'm here now, and I need to see you. It's important!

WOMAN Well, the rules say – oh, all right then.

The man sits down at the table, in front of the woman.

WOMAN Now how can I help you?

MAN Is this Room 365?

WOMAN Yes, it is.

MAN Good. Well, I'm here because of my monkey.

WOMAN Ah. Have you got a licence for it?

MAN No, that's why I'm here.

WOMAN Has the monkey got a number?

MAN Sorry?

WOMAN Did you get a ticket with a number for the monkey, when you came in?

MAN No, I didn't.

WOMAN There are two of you, so I need two numbers.

MAN Just a minute. (*He runs off and comes back with a ticket for the monkey.*) Here you are, then.

WOMAN Good. Now can you give me your PM624, please?

MAN Sorry, what's that?

WOMAN   A PM624? You write down the answers to a lot of questions about yourself and your monkey, on the PM624. It's very important.

MAN   Well, can you give me one, please?

WOMAN   No, I'm sorry, I can't.

MAN   Well, where can I get one, then?

WOMAN   Wait a moment, I must make a phone call. (*Telephoning*) Hello, Tom, it's Pam again. No, I'm at work. Can you bring a bottle with you when you come? All right. Goodbye, darling! (*To the man*) Right, now where were we?

MAN   A PM624?

WOMAN   Ah, yes. Well, have you got eight photos?

MAN   Eight photos?

WOMAN   Yes, four of you and four of the monkey.

MAN   Yes, I have. (*He gives her some photos.*)

WOMAN   Good. (*Looking at the photos carefully*) Wait a minute. These are very bad photos of you.

MAN   (*Looking at the photos, then laughing*) No, no! Those are the photos of the monkey! The other ones are the photos of me!

WOMAN   Ah, yes. Excuse me, I must make a quick phone call. (*Telephoning*) Hello, Tom. Pam here again. No, at the office. Shall we go to the cinema tonight? OK, I can get the tickets when I leave work. Goodbye, darling! (*To the man*) Right, now where were we?

MAN I'm waiting for a PM624.

WOMAN Ah, I see.

MAN Well, can I have one?

WOMAN Let me see, what day is it today?

MAN Tuesday. Why?

WOMAN Well, on Mondays, Wednesdays and Fridays you get PM624s from this office, but on Tuesdays and Thursdays you get them from Room 563.

MAN Room 563! Where's that?

WOMAN Oh, it's easy to find. Go out of the door. (*The man goes out.*) Go upstairs.

MAN (*Calling from offstage*) OK! What next?

WOMAN (*Taking down sign saying ROOM 365*) Go left, left and left again.

MAN (*Calling from offstage*) Right!

WOMAN Not right! Left, left and left again! Now come downstairs and it's the office on your right. (*She puts up a sign saying ROOM 563 on the wall.*)

MAN (*Coming in*) Hello. Oh, it's you.

WOMAN Hello, this is Room 563. Can I help you?

MAN But I was in this room just now. It's Room 365.

WOMAN No, it's Room 563. Look, it says ROOM 563 on the wall. Can I help you?

MAN I'd like a PM624, please.

WOMAN Good, good. Do sit down.

MAN   (*Sitting down*) But I don't understand!

WOMAN Well, you see, I'm doing the work of two people. I work in Room 365 and Room 563. So I put the two rooms together. It's easier for me.

MAN   Oh, I see. Well, can I have a PM624, please?

WOMAN Excuse me a minute. (*Telephoning*) Hello, Tom, Pam again. Yes, I'm going to be home soon. OK. See you soon. Goodbye, darling!

MAN   Can I have my PM624 now, please?

WOMAN Let me see. It's for this monkey, is it?

MAN   Yes, that's right.

WOMAN Is it a working monkey?

MAN   It doesn't do any work, no. It lives in my house.

WOMAN That's OK then, because for a working monkey the PM624 is no good at all.

MAN   (*Angrily*) Now look, are you going to give me that PM624 or not? I arrived here half an hour ago. First you told me to get a ticket, no, two tickets.

WOMAN Everybody needs a ticket. That's the rule.

MAN   (*More angrily*) Then you asked for eight photos. Then you told me to leave the room and come back again.

WOMAN To a different room. Room 563.

MAN   Now you're asking, is it a working monkey? And all the time you phone your friend Tom and talk about dinner and the cinema and...

'Can I have the PM624 now, please?'

He begins to cry.

WOMAN   I don't make the rules. I only work here, you know.

MAN   (*Feeling better*) Yes, I know. I'm sorry. Can I have
        the PM624 now, please?

WOMAN   Wait a minute. What's the time?

MAN   (*Looking at his watch*) One minute past five. Why?

WOMAN   Oh dear! This office closes at five. Can you come
        back tomorrow?

MAN   Aaaaargh! (*He runs off, crying.*)

INTRODUCTION

Gwen is Roger's girlfriend. She first met him ten years ago, and they go out together two or three times a week. Now she would like to marry him, but he never talks about marrying. This evening he's coming to dinner at her sister's beautiful house. Perhaps he's going to ask her to marry him tonight!

CHARACTERS IN THE PLAY

Gwen, a woman of about 30
Roger, a man of about 30

PERFORMANCE NOTES

The scene is a big living room, with expensive-looking chairs around a coffee table. There is a mirror on the wall. On the table there are some cigarettes and a woman's bag. Gwen is wearing a gold watch.
You will need some cigarettes, a cup of coffee and a ring.

Marry Me, Darling!

Gwen is looking at herself in the mirror.

GWEN (*To herself*) Mmm, you look beautiful! But what does Roger think? (*To the audience*) Roger's my boyfriend, you see. He's very shy, you know, and very poor. But perhaps tonight he's going to ask me to marry him. He's coming here to dinner at my sister's house. Nice, isn't it?

She looks around her, smiling. The door opens.

GWEN Ah, here he is!

Roger comes in.

ROGER (*Looking at her*) Oh, Gwen!

GWEN (*Looking at him*) Oh, Roger!

ROGER (*Moving nearer*) Oh, Gwen!

GWEN (*Looking at him*) Oh, Roger!

ROGER (*Moving nearer*) Oh, Gwen!

GWEN (*Looking away*) Oh, Roger! (*To the audience*) This is going to take all evening!

ROGER Gwen, my love.

GWEN (*Smiling at him*) Yes, Roger?

ROGER You know, we first met a long time ago.

GWEN Yes.

ROGER Nine years ago, I think.

GWEN   Ten!

ROGER   Sorry, of course it's ten. (*To the audience*) This isn't easy. She's very rich and I'm very poor. (*To Gwen*) Well, after ten years, it's time...

GWEN   (*Looking interested*) Yes?

ROGER   It's time...

GWEN   Yes?

ROGER   To have a cigarette, I think. Have you got one, Gwen?

GWEN   Of course, darling.

ROGER   (*To the audience*) What a wonderful house she's got! Everything in here looks very expensive.

She takes a cigarette from the table and gives it to him.

GWEN   Here you are, darling.

ROGER   (*Looking at her watch and speaking to the audience*) What a beautiful gold watch!

GWEN   What did you say, darling?

ROGER   Oh, it's your hands, darling. They're wonderfully, wonderfully beautiful!

GWEN   (*To the audience*) What's new about my hands? (*To Roger*) Oh Roger, you say the nicest things!

ROGER   And your mouth, Gwen...

GWEN   (*Coming nearer*) Yes, Roger?

ROGER   It's a beautiful flower – Oh! (*He moves quickly away, and Gwen puts her hand over her mouth.*)

GWEN   (*To the audience*) I had some garlic for lunch!

'Oh Roger, you say the nicest things!'

Roger, you're very handsome, you know.

ROGER (*Shyly*) Oh, am I, Gwen?

GWEN Oh yes. Your ears! I love your ears! They're very
– interesting. (*To the audience*) And very big.

ROGER Oh Gwen!

GWEN Your eyes! I love your eyes! They're very – blue.
(*To the audience*) And very cold.

ROGER Oh my love!

GWEN And your hair! I love your hair! It's very – brown.
(*To the audience*) There isn't much there.

ROGER Oh darling! Well, after that I must say …

GWEN Yes, Roger?

ROGER I need a coffee. Could you get me one, Gwen?

'Oh Roger, a ring! How beautiful!'

GWEN   Of course, darling. (*She goes out.*)

ROGER   (*To the audience*) I don't like milk in my coffee. Is she going to remember?

Gwen comes back and gives a cup of coffee to Roger.

GWEN   I put some milk in it, darling. Is that all right?

ROGER   Mmm, wonderful, darling. Just like you!

GWEN   (*Smiling shyly*) Oh Roger!

ROGER   Well, darling, it was eleven years ago…

GWEN   Ten!

ROGER   Of course. Ten. Ten. Sorry! So it's about time…

GWEN   Yes, darling?

ROGER   It's about time...

GWEN   Yes, darling?

ROGER   To bring you a little something.

He takes a ring from his pocket.

GWEN   Oh Roger, a ring! How beautiful!

ROGER   Do you like it? (*To the audience*) It was very expensive!

GWEN   Of course, darling. (*To the audience*) Oh dear, it looks so cheap. (*To Roger*). Roger, how exciting! Are you asking me...?

ROGER   Yes. (*Taking her hand*) Marry me, darling!

GWEN   Er, well, now you ask me, I don't know.

ROGER   You don't know?

GWEN   Well, this is all very sudden, Roger. I need some more time to think about it.

ROGER   (*To the audience*) Oh no! That's bad! I need her money. (*To Gwen*) How much time do you need?

GWEN   Well, I can give you an answer next week.

ROGER   But next week I'm going to New York!

GWEN   New York! How exciting!

ROGER   It's only for work, you know. (*To the audience*) Of course, Susie's going to be there! I always see her when I go to New York! (*To Gwen*) Oh Gwen! Please give me an answer before I leave!

GWEN   You see, Roger, you need to change a lot, before I can marry you.

ROGER   Change? Me? Change? But how?

GWEN   Well, to begin with, you must stop smoking!

ROGER   (*Looking at his cigarette*) Stop smoking?

GWEN   And you must stop drinking coffee!

ROGER   (*Looking at his coffee*) Stop drinking coffee?

GWEN   And you must stop going to New York, too!

ROGER   Stop going to New York? (*To the audience*) Does she know about Susie? Oh dear!

GWEN   So, Roger, what do you think? Can you change?

ROGER   What can I say, Gwen? I need you. (*To the audience*) And I need her money! (*To Gwen*) I'm going to stop smoking. And drinking coffee. And going to New York. (*To the audience*) Sorry, Susie!

GWEN   All right, Roger. I can give you my answer here and now. My answer is yes!

ROGER   Oh Gwen, darling!

GWEN   Oh Roger! (*They kiss.*)

ROGER   (*To the audience*) Now I needn't think about money any more! I'm going to have lots of money, my darling wife's money! (*Laughing*)

GWEN   (*To the audience*) Roger doesn't know this, but I'm not rich at all! I like expensive things, but I haven't got much money. When I tell him, what's he going to say? (*Laughing*)

They go out, hand in hand and smiling happily at each other.

GLOSSARY

actor a man who acts in plays or films

audience the people who listen to and watch a play

butler a man who works in another person's house, and takes special care of his employer's clothes, food and wine

café a snack-bar or small restaurant where you can buy drinks and snacks to eat

camping sleeping and cooking in the open air, as part of a holiday

crystal ball a large round glass ball, in which some people think they can see the future

dancing moving your arms and legs when you listen to music

darling a way of speaking to someone you love

film a moving picture that you see at the cinema or on television

future what is going to happen

garlic a plant used in cooking which makes your breath smell bad

gold yellow metal that is very expensive

gun a small metal weapon that shoots out bullets, to hurt or kill people

handsome (for a man) good-looking

holiday free time from work, or when you leave home to stay in a different place for a short time

kiss to touch someone with the lips in a loving way

licence a piece of paper showing that you are allowed to do something

marry to take someone as a husband or wife

mirror a piece of glass in which you can see yourself

plumber someone whose job is to put in and mend water pipes

poor of someone who hasn't got much money, the opposite of rich

ring a circle of metal, often gold, that you wear on your finger

rule what you must or must not do

shoot (past tense **shot**) to send a bullet from a gun to hurt or kill someone

shot the noise made by shooting

shy of someone who finds it difficult to talk to people and make friends

sir a polite way to speak to a man who is more important than you

sneeze to suddenly send out air from your nose and mouth

swimming pool a place built specially for swimming

travel agent someone whose job is to plan holidays for people

waiter a man who brings food or drinks to your table in a café

The Butler Did It
and Other Plays

ACTIVITIES

ACTIVITIES

Before Reading

1 Here are the six play titles. Which of the things, people or places below belongs to each play? Can you guess?

The Butler Did It   *Have a Nice Holiday!*   *Old Friends*
Rules are Rules   *Marry Me, Darling!*   *Fred's Future*

a waiter	a crystal ball	Hollywood
a travel agent	a box	a gun
a café	a monkey	New York
a gold watch	Spain	a bedroom

2 Read the back cover of the book, and the information on the first page. How much do you know now about the plays? Choose words to complete these sentences.

1 Perhaps someone's wife has a *brother / lover*.
2 There is a *cat / monkey* in one play.
3 Someone wants to *have a holiday / go shopping*.
4 James is a very *bad / good* butler.
5 Someone needs *a driving / an animal* licence.
6 One play has an *airport / office* worker in it.
7 Someone has a *beautiful daughter / rich girlfriend*.

3 Can you do this crossword? All the words are on the back cover or in the information on the first page.

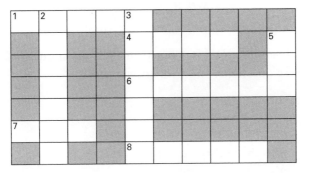

ACROSS

1 The opposite of expensive. (5)

4 What you must or must not do. (4)

6 A man who works in another person's house. (6)

7 A long way. (3)

8 To take someone as a husband or wife. (5)

DOWN

2 Free time from work. (7)

3 Something that is difficult; you need to find an answer. (7)

5 A polite way of speaking to a man. (3)

4 What is going to happen in some of the plays? Can you guess? Tick one box for each sentence.

YES   NO

1 James shoots his employer.

2 The man with the monkey gets his licence.

3 Roger asks his girlfriend to marry him.

While Reading

Read *The Butler Did It*. Choose the best question-words for these questions, and then answer them.

What / Who / Where

1 . . . is speaking to James on the phone?
2 . . . is in the bathroom at the moment?
3 . . . does Henry usually keep his gun?
4 . . . does Henry want James to do?
5 . . . does Henry say when James sneezes?
6 . . . does Henry think at the end of the play?

Read *Have a Nice Holiday!* Then put these sentences into the right order, to make a short paragraph of four sentences.

1 Mr and Mrs Boggis go to a travel agent,
2 So they go to Spain,
3 Florida is very expensive,
4 but they are not happy there.
5 the travel agent gives them tickets to Australia.
6 because they want to go on holiday.
7 and Antarctica is very cold.
8 When they come back,

Read *Old Friends*. Who said these words in the play?

1 'How wonderful to see you again!'

2 'What would you like?'

3 'There *is* a man in my life, and I'm going to marry him next week.'

4 'He asked me to call him Bob.'

5 'I'm his first girlfriend, you see.'

6 'Help! Help! Help!'

Read *Fred's Future*. Are these sentences true (T) or false (F)?

1 Rosa asks people for money when she tells them their future.

2 Fred has got a very nice American girlfriend.

3 Fred is going to shoot himself.

4 Rosa tells Fred his future three times.

5 The most important thing for Fred is to be famous.

Read *Rules are Rules* and *Marry Me, Darling!* Who did what in these plays? How many true sentences can you make?

The man with the monkey	drank some coffee.
	waited for half an hour.
The woman in the licence office	smoked a cigarette.
	changed the room number.
Gwen	phoned a friend.
Roger	said, 'Sorry.'
	had some garlic for lunch.
	looked in the mirror.

After Reading

1 Here are some new titles for the six plays. Which titles go with which plays? Some are better titles than others. Can you say why?

The Man with the Monkey   *Anyone for Tennis?*
Love is Everything You Need   *No Going Back*
One Man and Two Women   *Bless You, James!*

2 Perhaps the man with the monkey wrote his diary for the day when he went to the office. Join these halves of sentences together, using the words below to join them.

and   and then   because   but   so   when

  1 I went to the licence office

  2 First she told me to get a ticket,

  3 I had a very bad day today,

  4 In the end she closed the office

  5 Suddenly I got angry,

  6 I waited and waited in the office,

  7 ... she told me to go to another office.

  8 ... I feel very tired now.

  9 ... it was only one minute past five!

10 ... I wanted a licence for the monkey.

11 . . . the woman there didn't want to help.

12 . . . began to cry!

Now put the six sentences in the right order to make a paragraph.

3 Perhaps Celia had a talk with Robert later. Write out their conversation in the correct order, and put in the speakers' names. Celia speaks first (number 5).

1 _____: So that's the end for us, is it, Robert?

2 _____: Mandy? Yes, she's beautiful, and a wonderful dancer!

3 _____: Well! So you really like her?

4 _____: Well, yes, darling. And, er, can you give me back my ring? It *was* very expensive.

5 _____: Now Robert, what's all this about Amanda?

6 _____: Oh darling, with Mandy, it's different. She moves so well!

7 _____: Here it is. I never liked it. And stop calling me darling!

8 _____: Yes, I'm sorry, Celia darling, I do like her.

9 _____: But you don't like dancing!

10 _____: Do you know, I think – yes, I am, darling!

11 _____: Just tell me one thing – are you going to ask Amanda to marry you?

4 Perhaps this is what three of the characters in the plays are thinking. Which characters are they, and in which plays? What is happening in the play at the moment?

1 'Well, good luck to him. Everyone wants to be rich and famous, of course. And there are five more people waiting outside! Well, I know about *my* future – I'm not going to be famous, but I *am* going to be rich! Next, please!'

2 'Well, it's now or never. I must ask her tonight. Let's see, have I got the ring? Ah yes, in the top pocket. But what am I going to say? And what's her answer going to be?'

3 'What happened? Is she really dead? Did she have a lover? Or is he only the plumber – what was his name again? And what's going to happen to me, when someone finds their bodies? Or perhaps there aren't any bodies!'

5 Here is a puzzle. The answer is a word from *Old Friends* and *Marry Me, Darling!* with eight letters. To find the word, choose the right letters (one from each sentence) and write them in the boxes.

My first is in SHY.	☐	My fifth is in SANDWICH.	☐
My second is in WATCH.	☐	My sixth is in SCHOOL.	☐
My third is in BROWN.	☐	My seventh is in MILK.	☐
My fourth is in DINNER.	☐	My eighth is in EYES.	☐

You can say this about Robert, Bob, and Roger, but not usually about Celia, Amanda or Gwen. What is it?

6 Perhaps Mrs Boggis wrote a postcard from Australia to her sister. Use these words to complete it. (Use each word once.)

angry, breakfast, find, hot, laugh, pool, quiet, room, television, tickets, well

Dear Sue,

Here in Queensland it's very _____ at the moment. – 40C! So Trevor swims in the _____ most of the time. I'm sleeping _____ because the hotel is usually very _____. But last night the young man in the _____ next to us had his _____ on very late. And when Trevor spoke to him at _____, he got very _____. Really, these young people! So we're going to change our hotel today.

   Yesterday Trevor suddenly said, 'Where are our _____ home? I can't _____ them!' He does like a good _____! See you soon. Love, Linda

7 Which of these ideas do you agree (A) or disagree (D) with? Say why you agree or disagree.

1 It is wrong to have two girlfriends at the same time.
2 You must never kill anyone.
3 Nobody can see into the future.
4 Old school friends are always your best friends.
5 Everybody needs four weeks' holiday a year.
6 Nobody needs to have a butler these days.
7 Money is more important than love.

49

ABOUT THE AUTHOR

Bill (William) Bowler was born in London in 1957. As a child he loved singing, reading and acting, and first started writing plays when he was nine years old. After studying English Literature at Cambridge University, he studied mime with Marcel Marceau's teacher in Paris, and then trained as an English Language teacher. Since then he has been a writer, actor, director, editor, teacher and teacher trainer, and has worked in Europe, South America, Canada and the Far East. He now lives and works in the south-east of Spain with his wife, Sue Parminter, and their three children.

He has co-written *Headway Pronunciation*, *Network* and *Happy Earth* for Oxford University Press. He has also written seven graded readers for the OUP Dominoes series. His current job title is series editor (with Sue Parminter) of the Dominoes series.

Bill originally wrote *The Butler Did It* and the other plays in this book for his theatre group 'Original Travelling Theatre'. Comedy is what he specializes in. These plays have been performed in many different towns and to many different audiences. 'I know they work in practice,' Bill says, 'so I feel I want to share them with other people.'

OXFORD BOOKWORMS LIBRARY

Classics • Crime & Mystery • Factfiles • Fantasy & Horror
Human Interest • Playscripts • Thriller & Adventure
True Stories • World Stories

The OXFORD BOOKWORMS LIBRARY provides enjoyable reading in English, with a wide range of classic and modern fiction, non-fiction, and plays. It includes original and adapted texts in seven carefully graded language stages, which take learners from beginner to advanced level. An overview is given on the next pages.

All Stage 1 titles are available as audio recordings, as well as over eighty other titles from Starter to Stage 6. All Starters and many titles at Stages 1 to 4 are specially recommended for younger learners. Every Bookworm is illustrated, and Starters and Factfiles have full-colour illustrations.

The OXFORD BOOKWORMS LIBRARY also offers extensive support. Each book contains an introduction to the story, notes about the author, a glossary, and activities. Additional resources include tests and worksheets, and answers for these and for the activities in the books. There is advice on running a class library, using audio recordings, and the many ways of using Oxford Bookworms in reading programmes. Resource materials are available on the website <www.oup.com/bookworms>.

The *Oxford Bookworms Collection* is a series for advanced learners. It consists of volumes of short stories by well-known authors, both classic and modern. Texts are not abridged or adapted in any way, but carefully selected to be accessible to the advanced student.

You can find details and a full list of titles in the *Oxford Bookworms Library Catalogue* and *Oxford English Language Teaching Catalogues*, and on the website <www.oup.com/bookworms>.

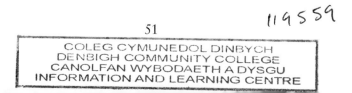

THE OXFORD BOOKWORMS LIBRARY
GRADING AND SAMPLE EXTRACTS

STARTER • 250 HEADWORDS

present simple – present continuous – imperative –
can/cannot, must – *going to* (future) – simple gerunds …

Her phone is ringing – but where is it?

Sally gets out of bed and looks in her bag. No phone. She looks under the bed. No phone. Then she looks behind the door. There is her phone. Sally picks up her phone and answers it. *Sally's Phone*

STAGE 1 • 400 HEADWORDS

… past simple – coordination with *and*, *but*, *or* –
subordination with *before*, *after*, *when*, *because*, *so* …

I knew him in Persia. He was a famous builder and I worked with him there. For a time I was his friend, but not for long. When he came to Paris, I came after him – I wanted to watch him. He was a very clever, very dangerous man. *The Phantom of the Opera*

STAGE 2 • 700 HEADWORDS

… present perfect – *will* (future) – *(don't) have to, must not, could* –
comparison of adjectives – simple *if* clauses – past continuous –
tag questions – *ask/tell* + infinitive …

While I was writing these words in my diary, I decided what to do. I must try to escape. I shall try to get down the wall outside. The window is high above the ground, but I have to try. I shall take some of the gold with me – if I escape, perhaps it will be helpful later. *Dracula*

… should, may – present perfect continuous – *used to* – past perfect –
causative – relative clauses – indirect statements …

Of course, it was most important that no one should see
Colin, Mary, or Dickon entering the secret garden. So Colin
gave orders to the gardeners that they must all keep away
from that part of the garden in future. ***The Secret Garden***

… past perfect continuous – passive (simple forms) –
would conditional clauses – indirect questions –
relatives with *where/when* – gerunds after prepositions/phrases …

I was glad. Now Hyde could not show his face to the world
again. If he did, every honest man in London would be proud
to report him to the police. ***Dr Jekyll and Mr Hyde***

… future continuous – future perfect –
passive (modals, continuous forms) –
would have conditional clauses – modals + perfect infinitive …

If he had spoken Estella's name, I would have hit him. I was so
angry with him, and so depressed about my future, that I could
not eat the breakfast. Instead I went straight to the old house.
Great Expectations

… passive (infinitives, gerunds) – advanced modal meanings –
clauses of concession, condition

When I stepped up to the piano, I was confident. It was as if I
knew that the prodigy side of me really did exist. And when I
started to play, I was so caught up in how lovely I looked that
I didn't worry how I would sound. ***The Joy Luck Club***

A Ghost in Love and Other Plays

MICHAEL DEAN

Do you believe in ghosts? Jerry doesn't. He's a nineteen-year-old American, who just wants a good holiday with his friend, Brad. They are travelling round the north of England by bicycle. But strange things begin to happen in the small hotel where they are staying. First, Brad seems to think that he has been there before. And then a girl called Ellen appears . . .

The first of these three original plays is set in the seventeenth century, and the other two take place in modern times. In each play, a ghost comes back from the dead to change the lives of living people.

Five Short Plays

MARTYN FORD

What do you do if you have a boring job in a restaurant, serving fast food to people who have no time to eat? Smile, and do your best? Perhaps it's better to find a place where time doesn't matter so much.

What if you dream of travelling to other countries, but your friends just laugh? Do you stay at home with them? Or do you decide to be more adventurous?

Perhaps you hear that someone has bought the last bag of salt in town. Do you buy a bag from him at a high price? Or try to make him give you a bag?

Our world is full of these kinds of problems. They make life interesting, and sometimes very funny. These five short plays show people trying to decide what to do in unexpected or difficult situations.

The Importance of Being Earnest

OSCAR WILDE

Retold by Susan Kingsley

Algernon knows that his friend Jack does not always tell the truth. For example, in town his name is Ernest, while in the country he calls himself Jack. And who is the girl who gives him presents 'from little Cecily, with all her love'?

But when the beautiful Gwendolen Fairfax says that she can only love a man whose name is Ernest, Jack decides to change his name, and become Ernest forever. Then Cecily agrees to marry Algernon, but only if his name is Ernest, too, and things become a little difficult for the two young men.

This famous play by Oscar Wilde is one of the finest comedies in the English language.

Hamlet

WILLIAM SHAKESPEARE

Retold by Alistair McCallum

Why does Hamlet, the young Prince of Denmark, look so sad? Why does he often say strange things? His family and friends are worried about him. Perhaps he is mad!

But Hamlet thinks that he has discovered a terrible secret about a recent crime in his family. Now he has no time for Ophelia, the sweet girl who loves him, or his friends, who were at school with him. He sits alone, and thinks, and plans. What will he decide to do? Will he ever be happy again?

This famous play by William Shakespeare, written in about 1600, is one of the finest in the English language.

Sister Love and Other Crime Stories

JOHN ESCOTT

Some sisters are good friends, some are not. Sometimes there is more hate in a family than there is love. Karin is beautiful and has lots of men friends, but she can be very unkind to her sister Marcia. Perhaps when they were small, there was love between them, but that was a long time ago.

They say that everybody has one crime in them. Perhaps they only take an umbrella that does not belong to them. Perhaps they steal from a shop, perhaps they get angry and hit someone, perhaps they kill . . .

Love among the Haystacks

D. H. LAWRENCE

Retold by Jennifer Bassett

It is hay-making time on the Wookey farm. Two brothers are building the haystack, but thinking about other things - about young women, and love. There are angry words, and then a fight between the brothers. But the work goes on, visitors come and go, and the long hot summer day slowly turns to evening.

Then the sun goes down, covering the world with a carpet of darkness. From the hedges around the hayfield comes the rich, sweet smell of wild flowers, and the hay will make a fine, soft bed . . .